W9-BFD-777

DONKEYS AND KINGS

Donkeys and Kings
. . . and other "tails" of the Bible

Written By Tripp York
Illustrations By Zak Upright

RESOURCE *Publications* • Eugene, Oregon

DONKEYS AND KINGS
And Other "Tails" of the Bible

Resource Publications
An imprint of Wipf and Stock Publishers
199 W. 8th Avenue, Suite 3
Eugene OR, 97401

ISBN 13: 978-1-60608-940-8

www.wipfandstock.com

To that remnant of West Burlington Church of the Nazarene who introduced me to a world of colorful stories filled with unforgettable characters.

Contents

But ask the animals, and they will tell you, the birds of the air, and they will tell you, ask the plants of the earth, and they will teach you, and fish of the sea will declare to you. Who among all these does not know that the hand of the Lord has done this? In his hand is the life of every living thing and the breath of every human being.
Job 12:7-10

As for the little donkeys of the New Testament, they are closer to angels than to people who are strong, powerful, and intelligent.
Andre Trocme

Acknowledgments

The French mathematician and philosopher Blaise Pascal claimed, "imagination decides everything." How we see the world determines how we will live in it, just as how we live in it will determine how we will see it. Our imaginations, therefore, play a significant role in how we live our lives. For many Jews and Christians, the Bible is the catalyst for how we see and, thus, live in the world. For this reason, I have attempted to imagine how non-human animals, those creatures created before us, very well might see their own place in this world—as well as in the kingdom to come. Though these are all fictionalized accounts, inspired primarily from scripture, I hope they allow for some re-imagining of God's place for all of us in God's peaceable kingdom.

The Bible contains a rather mixed account of animals. They are viewed at times as inherently good within themselves, and, at other times, their good is defined instrumentally by humans. Sometimes they are sacrificed, and sometimes they are protected from sacrifice. We are told not to eat them, and then we are told we can eat them. They often serve as companions, while other times they fear us as we fear them. Sometimes they save humans, and sometimes we save them. We are commanded to preach to them, and, just like humans, they occasionally listen.

Perhaps the only indisputable thing that can be said about animals is that they are a manifestation of God's creative wisdom. As they are creations of God, they deserve respect and care. The special privilege that humans have toward these non-humans is the ability to care for them and tell them who they are by how we treat them.

Though I do think it is a good thing that we are more attentive to the needs of our fellow creatures, this book is not an exercise in animal rights. Rather, this book is about the Kingdom of God and how all creatures are participants in this kingdom. The peaceable kingdom includes infants playing with snakes, wolves lying down with lambs, and donkeys conversing with prophets and kings. They are a part of our history, our tradition, and God's plans for a redeemed creation. For this reason, much of their behavior I highlight in this book does not always "make sense" unless we understand it through the lens of salvation history.

I am grateful to the Religion and Philosophy Departments at both Elon University and Western Kentucky University for their support and friendship. I owe an immense debt of gratitude to my editor, an Elon University graduate, Lesley Tkaczyk. Granted, I stubbornly ignored her advice to exclude chapter seven; nevertheless, I fear ever having to write a book without her aid. Hopefully, I can convince her to continue working with me.

Zak Upright's illustrations are astonishing and add a beauty and richness impossible with words alone. I hope to collaborate on future projects. Holly Williford-Upright did an amazing job providing the set-up and layout to complete this fantastic literary labor of love. Many thanks to resident zoologist Carly Sinderbrand who made sure I did not make any glaring mistakes in my more detailed discussions about the various species found in this book. How else would I be able to talk about marsupials and monotremes in an intelligible manner if not for her scholarship?

Finally, this book would be impossible if not for those people who introduced me to the odd and peculiar stories that constitute scripture. Many thanks to the Goodes, Gantos, Faucettes, Fields, Faulkners, Seays, Thomases, Copelands, Burkes, Wagners, Gammons, Middendorfs, Wilkinsons, Yorks, and Kroezes that were my first church family. The introduced me to a world of stories that pursue me wherever I go.

1
The King's Spider

In a country far away, at a time not
entirely different from our own,
existed a spider of no great significance. Her name was Sadie, and, just
like other spiders, she had tiny little
fangs, spinnerets that produced silk
of great strength, and was blue-
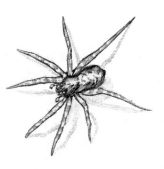
blooded. She had a silver stomach and eight long striped legs. She
was quite proud of her markings, even though she was well aware
that her mother, and her mother's mother before her, and all of
their mothers before them, shared these same characteristics.
Sometimes this made her proud, while other times she longed for
a life set apart from those like her. Such longing was noticeably
absent in other spiders, which made her question why she should
suffer alone in her hope for something more.

Why couldn't she simply accept the life she had been
given? Why did she feel troubled to want more than what was possible?

This was not, however, the root cause of her frequent bouts
with unhappiness. You see, despite being altogether lovely, strong
and agile, she was a spider who was all too familiar with what some
have deemed "the great sadness."

Sadie was heartbroken.

It began in her youth when she caught a glimpse of a beautiful young boy cavorting with his friends in the fields of Aurum.
His untroubled face, his carefree approach to life, and the wonder

of his smile enchanted her. She was completely, without reservation, and for all intents and purposes, smitten. It was not, however, a superficial attraction. His dark eyes matched by his dark hair matched by his dark golden skin, played only a small role in her love for him. It was the stories, the adventures and the magnificent life he lived, that drove her to the brink of lovesick madness.

After she first saw him at play in the fields, she tried her best to follow his life. She desperately wanted to know everything about him. This was not terribly difficult, as his actions quickly became legendary. With each passing day his heroism seemed to rise above life. On more than one occasion he successfully fought, barehanded no less, both a lion and a bear to save the life of a small lamb. The mere thought of it all was quite incredible to Sadie.

One might say his greatest achievement, however, was his battle against the giant from Gath. Some claim that this colossal warrior was the result of a misguided union between angels and humans. Of that, I do not presume to know. What I do know is that he was so big, so massive, that he had to have special clothes made for him. This, unfortunately, made him feel superior to everyone else, and he used his enormous size to bully those he did not like—including the object of Sadie's affection. Yet, the spider's love stood his ground and easily defeated the once terrifying giant.

While others were shocked at the outcome, Sadie was not in the least bit surprised. It seemed as though there was nothing her love could not do—except notice the undying adoration of one lone spider. Then again, why should he, thought Sadie. He was, after all, a slayer of giants, a friend to the weak and to the defenseless. He was also an able musician, a talented poet capable of creating sounds and sonnets that weakened even the toughest of knees. He was larger than life, while her kind, if even noticed, seemed to only be a nuisance to those with two legs. She was, after all, just a spider. What could she do of any real significance? She could never defeat a giant. A lamb would be foolish to seek her help against a lion or a bear. She did not know how to play any instruments or write poetry. She could only weave webs capable of ensnaring tiny insects. How that pales in comparison, imagined Sadie, to even the smallest of her loves' many amazing deeds.

Time went by rather slowly for the sad spider. Days became weeks and weeks became months, as tends to be the case. Sadie was moving well beyond her youth. Spiders age considerably faster than those with two legs, and she had already lived through six seasons. She did not know how many more she would live to see.

Fall was her favorite. The birds that give her so much trouble during the spring and summer begin to move elsewhere; they do not enjoy the cold that late fall ushers in. Of course, Sadie was not a fan of the cold either, so as her second winter approached she sought a new home. Upon the advice of an old friend, Sadie retreated from the adventures of her unrequited love, as well as the everyday chaos of life in the open, and sought peace and solitude in an abandoned cave overlooking her beloved fields. The cave originally housed a very large bear notorious for hunting sheep.

One morning, not so long ago, the bear left on a hunt, never to return. Sadie once knew all the details, but had long since forgotten them. Old age is rarely kind to the memory.

Food in the cave was far scarcer than she had imagined. Of course, it was taking her longer and longer to weave her webs, and she noticed that they were not quite as strong as they had once been. Though she no longer desired to leave the comfort of her new home, necessity required that she occasionally venture out to a nearby oak in hopes of finding food.

As she made her way out of the mouth of the cave, she paused in order to look at the fields that had once hosted many grand adventures. She looked out over the browning fields—the rainbow of colors had long since passed. This brought her no great deal of joy, as she loved to bask in the sun and the multiplicity of colors provided by the numerous blossoms of early spring. Though she would never again live amidst the flowers, as her old age made her much too slow to avoid the hungry birds, she hoped that she would live long enough to be able to look, just once more, at the spectrum of beauty created by rain and warm air. Moreover, she thought about the boy who captured her imagination and had, unwittingly, caused her much joy and sadness. For a brief moment, Sadie forgot why she ventured out of the cave. Her rumbling stomach reminded her.

Sadie spent all morning and afternoon searching for food. Web after web was spun, but when she came back to check them, they were either empty or broken. Today would be yet one more day without food. Sadie would spend another long night hoping against hope that the next day would prove to be better.

She made her way back home knowing that, unless something changed, she would die there. The cave often reminded her of how alone she was, and Sadie did not like that feeling. She had hundreds of brothers and sisters, yet time had divided them. Her cold and damp home was all that she had. Maybe, she forced herself to think, tomorrow would be better.

As she settled in, she faintly heard the breathing of another creature in the cave. It was coming from the very back. Had the bear returned? As she moved closer, the breathing sounded heavier and panicked. Then she heard a voice. It was the voice of one who walks on two legs. She could not make out everything it was saying: something about the "uselessness" of something or another. Sadie's ears were not quite what they used to be, nor was her eyesight, because the closer she moved to the voice the more and more it looked like, like . . . it . . . was . . . him. It was the one whom she had spent her entire life loving, and here he was in her cave! But why? He lived in a palace with fine foods and clothing. Why would he be here? And why was he so frantic, so upset? He appeared almost frightened and unsure of himself. This seemed like a very different person from the one who bested giants and wrote lovely poetry, but this was indeed the same young man. He was sitting with his knees to his chest, arms covering his face, cowering in the back of the dark cave going on and on about "why this?" and "why that?" when it suddenly dawned on Sadie that he was hiding.

Someone wanted to do him harm.

For what reason, she could scarcely imagine. Why would anyone want to hurt him? She did not know, nor did she think this was the time to speculate; rather, this was a time for action.

At that very moment, something in Sadie returned— something she thought had long since passed. It was as if her whole life had led up to this one defining moment, and she could not bear the thought of failure. But what could she do? She was but a mere spider. The two-legged ones trample on her kind without so much as a thought, many times without even trying. What could she possibly do? Doubt filled her head and notions of insignificance plagued her as she clung to the surface of the cave wall. There was only one thing a spider like herself could do: build webs. What use it would be to him, she did not know, but she knew something must be done. Suddenly, she had an idea. If someone were after him, she would (for she must), build the biggest and strongest web of her life, and she must do it now.

Taking one last look at her love, she quickly turned and raced back to the entrance of the cave. Once she arrived, she put her plan into motion. She began spinning web, as quickly as she could, as much as she could. She crossed left and right, up and down, in circles, zig-zagging, doing everything she could to make the finest web she had ever created. The strain it was placing on her was great, but she could not let him down. She kept going. All night, without ever stopping, with not so much as a bit of food in her stomach, she sealed the entrance of the cave with the biggest, most beautiful web that this world has ever seen. Finally, she was finished. She had no more silk to weave. Her body was depleted. She collapsed on the ground, as she was too weak to even cling to the top of her own web.

As she lay there, exhausted and weary, she saw a number of others two-legged creatures walk up to the cave. They tried to look in, but her web served as a shield against sight into her home—into his hiding place. One of them pulled out a large, sharp object. Sadie was terrified that it was going to be used to slice through her defenses, but at the last second one of the others said something, the content of which she is not sure, and they, fortunately, left.

Sadie continued lying on the ground. Though she was worn out, she no longer felt alone, hungry, or, more importantly, without purpose. A feeling of warmth consumed her body. She had never been so happy. She was significant.

That spring, the trees blossomed and the flowers bloomed.

2
Twenty-Two Hands

"Tell it again! Come on, please!"

The young foal pleaded with her great grandfather to re-peat the story. It really was quite the miracle. Not just the story, but the fact that Jack had great grandchildren, or even grandchildren for that matter.

The odds were certainly stacked against old Jack, yet he had lived a life of miracles. He was noted for saying, "Well, I never thought that would happen!" so often that neighbors told him to just stop "thought-ing." So he did. Jack was not much of a thought-er, or a, um, thinker, but he didn't have to be. He was Jack. And Jack wouldn't have been who he was today if he had always thought everything through.

"Oh, come on!"

She was whining now.

She was such a pro at whining.

Jack was a softie, so, of course, he was going to tell the story . . . again. But he was also tired. He had lived a long life and seen many unusual things. It wasn't that he didn't enjoy telling the story; he just wasn't sure why everyone thought it was such a big deal. I mean, what was he supposed to do? He did what any other sensible donkey would have done: he stood his ground. Jack was always good at standing his ground. "It's a certain trait that's indicative of being a donkey," Jack was fond of saying. He had no idea what "indicative" meant, but he heard his friend Ludwig say it once, and Ludwig sounded like he knew what he was talking about.

Ludwig is a lion.

Donkeys and lions don't always make the best of friends, but, as I said, Jack lived a life of miracles. I guess, in a way, so did Ludwig. After all, one of his best friends was a donkey. How many lions can claim that?

So, Jack consented to tell the story. How could he not? His great, and I do mean great, granddaughter was a cutie. She used such cuteness to her advantage. That makes her clever.

Cute and clever.

Sometimes clever is good.

Sometimes it isn't.

But, in Jack's eyes, it was hard to find anything wrong with his little Jenny. Honestly, do you know the odds against a Jack even having a Jenny? They're terrible, I'll have you know. Terrible.

Not good at all.

You see, Jack's granddaughter Winnie was a hinny. Hinny's rarely have Jenny's. Jenny, who came from a hinny, Jack sometimes joked, "was a plenty." And she was a being a plenty right now.

But there she was. Against all the odds, there she was. Asking her great grandfather to tell the story, again, for only the, oh, let's see, only the . . .

"How many times have I told you this story, Jenny?"

"Oh, I don't know," she answered rather playfully. "Just a few times."

"Ha!" shrieked Jack. "If by a few times you mean 'about a hundred,' then I guess it has been just a few times."

Jack was being a bit clever himself.

Jenny pinned back her ears.

Oh no, thought Jack, here it comes. "Okay, okay, okay," he interrupted, "please, no whining. You whine like your mother. Whew."

She boasted, "I'll take that as a compliment."

Yep, she was a cute one.

Jack wandered over to his stall, grabbed a carrot, offered his great granddaughter a bite (she politely declined) and began:

"All right, so, we were going to—"

"Wait a second Poppy." (That's what foals call their great grandfathers—poppy. It's a well known fact.) "You can't start there!"

"Who's telling the story?" asked Jack.

Except, since he had a carrot in his mouth, it sounded more like "Who fell in with shorty?"

"What?" asked Jenny.

"What?" repeated Jack.

"Nothing. I just don't know why you insist on eating carrots when you tell your stories."

Great grandchildren, thought Jack. He had to keep reminding himself: miracle. "Okay, okay, I've finished eating the carrot. So where were we?"

Jenny pondered for a moment, and then asked, "What comes before the beginning?"

"What comes before the beginning?" repeated Jack. "Well, um, I don't know. That's a really good question. I don't know that anything comes before the—oh, I get it."

Miracle.

Just keep think-ing miracle.

"As I was saying, we were heading out for quite the journey. I was

all saddled up and carrying more than my fair share, as usual."

Here it comes, thought Jenny.

"Horses have it easy compared to us," Jack went on. "They prance around like they own the place, but it's us donkeys that carry the weight of the world. Without us where would anyone be? Yessiree, we bear the burden of the world."

Getting sidetracked was common place when old Jack told a story. You just had to wait it out.

Jenny would occasionally help him a little, "So, you were all saddled up and—"

"Yeah, okay. We were all saddled up and Mr. B. hopped on. Did I mention that he had put on a few pounds in the—"

"Poppy!"

"Sheesh. I thought you liked details. It's all about the details you know?"

Jenny's ears were starting to pin back.

"Right, so, moving forward. Mr. B. hopped on and we headed out to talk to some pretty important officials. I can't quite recall where they were from; I just know they were pretty important. They wore important clothes. You know, the kind of clothes people who ride fancy horses wear. Horses. Pfft. As if they are—"

"HEEHAW!!!" screamed Jenny, at what must have been a thousand decibels louder than any creature should ever be allowed to scream.

"Ooouuucchh Jenny! Ow. You bray like no other donkey on the planet. You see these ears?" he asked as he wiggled them around on his head. "They're huge. I think you broke them."

And just as if she were the most innocent and most blameless creature on the planet she softly said, "Story, please."

"Do you promise never to do that again, Jenny?"

"Nope. Mom says not to make promises." But, seeing that her great grandfather was nearing the edge she added with the slyest grin ever, "But I'll certainly try."

"Fair enough," said Jack. "Where were we? Oh, yes. So, we were heading out to meet with some pretty important people and as we were making our way down the road we came across this guy carrying a sword."

"What did it look like?" interrupted Jenny.

"What? The sword? Oh, it was big. Really big. It was very shiny, and looked quite sharp. I have to be honest, I was a little worried. He just stood there staring at us and I thought at any time he was going to pounce on Mr. B. But do you know what Mr. B. wanted to do?"

"Walk right to him," answered Jenny.

Oblivious to the fact that she answered his question Jack said, "Walk right to him."

"So, what did you do?"

"Well, I certainly didn't want any part of that. I had served Mr. B. for a long time and I didn't want to see either one of us get hurt. So, I strayed off the path. And guess what Mr. B. did?"

"He hit you!" squealed an excited Jenny.

"He hit me. Can you believe that? That guy with the sword must have been at least 22 hands tall, and Mr. B. hit me for trying to avoid him."

"What did you do next?"

"Well, I got off the road anyway. I was more worried about the guy with the sword than Mr. B. So, I took him down a different path. One that I hoped would be safer. We cut across to this vineyard—you know how much I love grapes, right? Ahhh, when they are at their ripest I could eat them until the cows come home. And you know how late cows stay out don't you?"

"Poppy?"

"Yes?"

"I'm trying over here," Jenny pleaded. "I am really, really trying."

Jack knew that look and didn't think his ears could take the punishment. "Oh good heavens, yes, on with the story. Well, there was this narrow little path with a wall on both sides and I thought that if we could escape through there we would be safe, but guess who was there waiting for us?"

"Mr. 22-hands sword guy?"

"Can you believe it? It was Mr. 22-hands sword guy! Silly Mr. B. wanted to go right toward him again. So, I thought I would give Mr. B. a wake-up call."

"What did you do?" asked Jenny.

"I just sort of ever-so-slightly ran his leg into the wall."

"Ha-ha!" shouted Jenny. "Oh, what great fun you must have been having!"

"It was not fun at all, I'll have you know. And I didn't want to hurt Mr. B. I wanted to save him . . . and, sure, possibly my own hide, but I was just looking out for his best interests. I mean, was he blind or something? It was right there in front of him."

"Maybe his eyes just weren't as good as yours," offered Jenny.

"Well, I don't how bad they would have to be to not see him, so I just figured that Mr. B. had lost his mind rather than his eyesight."

"What did he do when you hurt his leg?"

"You'll never guess in a million years," said Jack.

Jenny quickly belted, "He hit you again!"

"He hit me again." With a deep reflective sigh Jack pondered, "What keeps a donkey like me going I ask you? What keeps me going?"

After about three seconds, what seemed to Jenny to be an infinity of nothingness, (what Jack would refer to as a pause for dramatic effect), she cunningly asked, "Surely that's not the end of the story, Poppy?"

"No, no, of course not, that's not the end of the story. We took a different path; this one was even more narrow than the previous one. I was thinking that perhaps Mr. 22-hands sword guy wouldn't be able to follow us on such a treacherously thin trail. But, low and behold, if I were to give you a hundred guesses you would never guess what happened next."

"He got in front of you again!"

"He got in front of us again. It was truly unbelievable."

Jenny's heart was racing with excitement. "So, what did you do?"

"Well, what could I do? The path was so narrow that I couldn't turn either right or left so . . ."

"So . . ." responded an anxious Jenny. "What did you do?! What did you do?!"

And with a look of absolute satisfaction, Jenny's hero, and the hero for donkeys, mules and hinnies of generations to come, responded with his incredible tactic for dealing with power and adversity: "I did the only thing any good self-respecting donkey could do in a situation like that," after inserting a slight pause for dramatic effect, Jack continued, "I sat down."

"Ah, you sat down!" Jenny wailed approvingly.

As if to drive the point home, Jack reiterated, almost like a sigh, how he saved his master's life: "I sat down."

"Brilliant," whispered Jenny. "Absolutely brilliant."

After a moment or two, which gave them plenty of time to think about the gravity of the situation, Jack said, "Well, Mr. B. didn't think so. To be honest, he was rather angry with me. He had an important meeting to get to and I was keeping him from it. Or, at least, so he thought."

"So what did he do next?" she asked tentatively.

"Well, I hesitate to tell you this, for no foal should be subject to hearing about such cruelty, but—"

"He hit you with his staff!" interrupted Jenny.

"He hit me with his—hey, you don't have to sound so excited about it!" protested her great grandfather.

"Oh, I'm not. We're just getting to my favorite part is all."

"Okay," said Jack, who was not quite fully trusting of her intentions. "Well, by this point I had enough. I looked straight at Mr. B. and said, 'What have I done to you, that you have struck me these three times?'"

"Wow. Mom told me to never talk to humans, no matter what! Weren't you scared of what would happen?"

"Of course I was sca—I mean, no, not at all. Your mother is right by the way. It's far better to keep our tongues to ourselves when it comes to communicating with humans. It's not as if we don't already understand them without speech, but sometimes when we talk to them, well, they just don't understand."

"Silly humans," muttered this proud daughter of a hinny.

"Well, now, go easy on them. We were here long before they were, at least a half a day or so; they still have a lot to learn."

Jenny vocalized, "I know, I know," even though she was still thinking "silly humans."

"Anyway," Jack continued, "after I asked him why he hit me three times he said it was because I made a fool out of him. He even threatened to hurt me if he could just find a sword. It was at this point, by the way, that I did not think it wise to bring up the guy standing in front of us. I didn't want to give Mr. B. any ideas."

"Well, what did you say to that?"

"I said, 'Mr. B., am I not your donkey, which you have ridden all of your life until this very day? Have I been in the habit of treating you this way?' That's what I said to him. Sure as I am standing right here in front of you, that's what I said to him. And do you know what he said Jenny?"

"No."

"Yep, he said 'no.'"

A confused look washed over Jack's face. "Wait, were you saying 'no' because you didn't know what he said, or were you saying that he said 'no'?"

"Did he say 'no'?"

Jack slowly answered, "Yes."

"Ha! Okay!" laughed the cunning foal.

"Right . . . well, he said 'no.'" Jack thought it was a good time to get back on track. "And then, all of a sudden, out of nowhere, it was as if Mr. B. saw this guy with the sword for the first time. Mr. B. dropped to the ground and fell on his face. Then, Mr. 22-hands sword guy asked him the same thing I asked, except with a loud, booming voice perfect for a person of that stature: 'WHY DID YOU STRIKE YOUR DONKEY THREE TIMES?'"

Jenny loved that part. Jack did a great impression of Mr. 22-hands sword guy.

"Did he say anything else? Anything at all?" she excitedly asked.

"The most interesting thing, I'll have you know. He told Mr. B. that if it were not for me, he would have killed him and let me go on about my merry way. Can you believe that? I saved Mr. B.'s life! Me. A donkey. A donkey saved his life."

"Yes," confirmed Jenny, "exactly." And in a voice that suggested she was more talking to herself than her great grandfather she said, "It's just almost too good to be true."

Jenny sighed, but quickly recovered from her "Jack moment." (Anytime you talk to yourself while someone else is around it's called a "Jack moment.") "Then what happened?" she asked.

"Well, to be honest, I'm not entirely sure. Mr. B. started talking about how he had been blind, but that was news to me. He sure had no problem finding my backside when he wanted to hit it. But, anyway, he said he was sorry countless times and, well, it ended with our little family getting a lifetime supply of carrots and oats."

With what sounded like speech delivered at the speed of light, Jenny burst in with the greatest sense of urgency: "Oh, Poppy, you make it sound so easy. I don't know if I would have had the courage to do what you did. I'm sure I wouldn't have had the courage. Who would have had the courage? You would have to be crazy to have that kind of courage! I mean, were you not worried that Mr. B was going to hurt you? I would have been worried that Mr. B would hurt me. It is certainly no fun to get hurt. Weren't you worried?"

Jack tried to interrupt, but with no such luck.

"He's a very well respected person, you know? Of course you know. He knows lots of people and everybody is always trying to get him to pay them a visit and mom says that you were the only one who ever said 'no' to him and you did that three times and mom sometimes wonders what made you do it and I don't know what made you do it. Why did you do it? I just don't see how you did it."

She finally took a breath.

"So, how did you do it?"

Jack looked at his sweet little Jenny. Sure, she was full of bravado and spunk, but that's part of what it means to be a foal. So much show goes into these little creatures, and Jenny was no different—except that she was his little miracle. As he stood there thinking about it, Jack wondered what was the bigger of the two miracles: That he would have a granddaughter who was a hinny give birth to "Jenny the plenty," or, that he sat down when Mr. B. demanded that he keep walking. He didn't quite know. All he knew was that the more he thought about it, the more he thought he shouldn't be a thoughter, or a, um, thinker.

Fortunately, Jenny disturbed his thoughten' with a big ear to ear grin: "It's good to be a donkey, huh Poppy?"

"It's the best," replied Jack. "Now, how about we have a carrot or two? I had to sit down to get these, you know?"

This time, Jenny gladly accepted the offer of a free carrot that had been heroically earned by her great, and I do mean great, grandfather.

3
Hunger Strike

"I'm not about to eat that."

"Me either!" squealed the small cub.

"Did you hear that Linus?" asked Lucy. "That's your very own pride talking. Are you happy now?"

"Of course I'm not happy, Lucy. Ever since they stuck us in here we've become exactly what they want us to become, exotic pets. We're nothing more than domesticated cats that eat when they tell us to eat and jump when they tell us to jump. I'm telling you, this is no life for a lion. Do you think they would be happy if we put them in a cage and fed them on our own time? Kept them around for our own amusement? Made them do tricks to impress our friends? I don't think so."

"But Linus—"

"No 'buts' about it Lucy, this is no life for us. I'm not about to just lay down here and be their little pet. Nor will I allow my family to exist for no other reason than to make the king's court happy."

"That is exactly the kind of talk that landed us in here in the first place," exclaimed Lucy's older sister Lilly. "Had we been a bit more cooperative on the outside maybe we wouldn't even be here. Plus, the way I see it, this life is much easier than out there. Sure, we may have been free before, but in here we never have to worry about food, the weather, or hyenas. I don't have to remind you what happened to Luke, do I?"

"If I ever get my paws on those . . . ", Linus growled.

"Well, you won't," interrupted Lilly, "so try not to get your mane all in a knot. Just be happy you don't ever have to worry about that happening to sweet little Leo. If that were to happen to him, well, I'm just saying I will take this kind of life over the so-called 'wild' any day of the week."

"I wanna be wild! I wanna be wild!" Leo shouted as he ran in circles.

"Child, you are wild. No worries there," said his mother Lucy. "Listen, who's to say which life is better? I don't know. All I do know is that my cub is hungry, and I'm going to feed him."

"Well put, Lucy," said her sister. "At least the meat our keepers gave us this time is fresh. You have to be thankful for that Linus."

"Keepers?" the lion muttered under his breath. "More like kidnappers."

The sisters slowly walked toward their dinnertime meal. They had been without food for two days now and decided that while debates on freedom were important, they were not as important as eating. Food always comes at a price, and this situation, so thought the lionesses, was no different.

"Wait," said Linus.

Lilly quickly turned to him, "I'm not about to delay my—"

"Just wait a second, okay? If we're going to eat this poor excuse for a meal we should at least find out what it did to deserve being here in the first place."

"I'm sure it wasn't anything too exciting," declared Lucy. "They send one another down here for the silliest reasons."

"Well, when you think you own the whole planet," said Linus, "it's easy to fight over the most trivial things. They spend so much of their time bullying each other, bullying us, and every other creature on this earth, that it just comes natural for them to assume life is nothing more than one big fight. They do whatever they want whenever they want to whomever they want just to make themselves happy. If they have to kill, eat, or cage us in the process, so it goes, I guess."

"On that point, you may be right sweetheart," agreed Lucy. "After all, I thought they were supposed to take care of the earth and all its inhabitants, not abuse them."

"What's wrong with you?" asked a stunned Lilly. "You're starting to sound just like him."

"She doesn't sound like me," shouted Linus, defensively. "I don't need them to take care of me. I was doing just fine before their kind ever showed up, and I imagine we will do much better once they're gone."

With a bit of sorrow in her heart, Lucy looked toward her mate and said, "Oh, my dear, dear husband. We must all share this place together. Maybe it is up to us to show them the way." Lucy stared into the eyes of her beloved for a moment, then looked at their food and said, "Lilly, perhaps Linus is right. Not necessarily about us going on a hunger strike, but, perhaps we should not jump so hastily into this meal. Maybe we could at least see why he's down here."

"You two are simply crazy," mumbled Lilly. "You're both living in some dream world which does not, nor ever will, exist."

Lilly looked at the two of them to make sure they were actually serious about engaging in conversation with their food before eating it. She had seen that determined look of both her sister and her brother-in-law before and knew arguing about it was useless. She gave in, at least temporarily.

"Fine. Go find out why they served us one of their own," Lilly said. "But I'm telling you now, he's got about five minutes to live, and then he's mine."

Lilly turned around and walked to the back of the den. Though the den was quite small in size, it was tall enough to keep the lions captive. It was slightly square in shape, very stuffy, and a bit dark as it contained only one small opening for light. This was strategically placed at the tallest part of the den where food would be lowered, or dropped, to the lions. Despite having such powerful legs, there was no chance any of them would ever be able to jump out of it. This was, of course, purposeful. It wouldn't be very good to have a couple of lions roaming around the town. Lilly, however, wasn't concerned with ideas of escape, she just wanted to eat. As she settled down with her back to the others she reiterated, "Five minutes."

Lucy and Linus slowly approached the rather frail human who had remained silent during the lions' heated dispute. Although lions have little understanding of the life expectancy of caged humans (or humans in the wild for that matter), this one seemed to be up in years; he was an older man. For some reason, which both of them were not quite sure of, they didn't want to scare him.

Leo cautiously stayed behind his mother. He was desperately curious, but also a bit wary. He had never seen a human up-close before, and, because of the stories his father told, he was not terribly eager to meet one. Yet this particular one, the young cub thought, seemed different from those in his imagination. It would be many years later before he would be able to explain why or how, but for now, he just knew that this one was unique.

As the three approached their would-be meal, Linus sat down in front of him and asked, "Beyond the obvious reason, why exactly did they throw you to us?"

"Linus," Lucy calmly reprimanded, "where are your manners?" Reminding him of proper feline etiquette she said, "We must first introduce ourselves."

Looking at the old man, and extending a paw, she introduced her family.

"Hello. My name is Lucy. The grumpy one here, who, by the way, may be your best friend at the present moment, is my dearest husband Linus."

As she introduced him, she nestled her nose in his dark mane (as was her habit when trying to show him that the world was not so bad).

"This is our little one," she continued. "His name is Leo, and the one back there, the one salivating, that's Lilly. She's planning on eating you in about four minutes. Oh, sorry, that probably didn't help calm your nerves, did it?"

"Not really," said the elderly man.

"Nevertheless," continued Lucy, "it is a pleasure to meet

you. Where is your territory?"

"Territory?" asked the man. "I guess, originally, that would be Judah, but I have been in the service of various kings in this province for many, many years."

Almost jumping out of his skin, Leo shouted from behind his mother, "So, what did you do to end up in here with us? I mean, you must have really angered the king something fierce! What'd you do? What'd you do?"

"Leo," his mother said gently, "what did I tell you about interrupting?"

Sheepishly retreating, the cub apologized, "Sorry mom. And, um, sorry sir."

The old man, who was not noticeably bothered by the young cub's eager questions, told him, "Oh, it's okay. I don't mind. But, to answer your question, and your father's as well, I didn't anger the king at all. We're actually friends."

Casting looks of confusion to one another, the lions stared, in a rather puzzled manner, back at the old man as if his claim of kingly friendship was given in an meaningless language. This went on for a few moments until a lone voice in the background cut in: "Three minutes."

"I guess we better make this quick then, huh?" smiled Lucy. "So, if you are friends with the king, how did you end up in here? I thought the king was in charge of, well, pretty much everything."

"Yes, that's partially true," stated the old man. "However, he's not above the law—even if he's the one who created it."

Realizing that the lions were not quite sure of what he was saying, and that he had precious few minutes left to live, he added, "To make a long story short, the king created a law that demanded something I couldn't give. He wasn't really even aware of what he was doing, at least not fully aware, and, as you might guess, disobedience to the law—even if it is for a higher authority—sometimes gets you thrown in a lion's den."

As if he were completely confused, Linus asked, "What, for you human animals, is higher than the law? You die for laws, kill for laws, you imprison people, as well as other animals, in the name of the law! What could possibly be higher than the laws in whose name you do these things?"

"Contrary to what some lawmakers think, human laws are not the highest law. I imagine, for very different reasons, you lions would agree. Though human laws can be good, they can also be quite bad. When this happens, sometimes the best way to show others a law is not right is to break it."

"Even at the expense of your own life?" sneered Lilly. During the course of the conversation, no one had noticed Lilly slowly making her way over until she was but a few feet, or one good pounce, away from her meal.

"Say, that was a quick three minutes," he nervously offered.

"I asked you a question, sir. Are there laws worth breaking, worth ignoring, even at the expense of your own life?"

The man gazed at the eldest of the lions in the den. Though she was in the twilight of her years, she still commanded an intimidating presence. He then looked at the small cub sitting behind his much larger mother, peering up at him with his big brown eyes. He wasn't sure if the cub was staring at him all wide-eyed out of fear or amazement. Either way, for the briefest of moments, he envied his innocence.

Once it's lost, he thought to himself, it's never coming back.

He turned his attention to Lucy. Here was a hunter in her prime. She seemed to be understanding, perhaps even a bit sympathetic, of his plight, yet she was a hunter all the same. He had to respect that fact. She is who she is.

Finally, his eyes made their way to Linus. Here was a king, in his own right, struggling to maintain his dignity while reduced to receiving handouts from a species that had belittled his kind. It can't be easy for him.

After surveying those who surrounded him, he turned his attention back to Lilly and, with an odd sort of courage not to be confused with arrogance, responded: "You want to know if I think there are laws worth disobeying at the expense of one's own life? Look at me. Look where I am. I trust that my presence down here with you answers that question."

The old lioness, ripe with wisdom (for she had experienced much in her lifetime), gave him a look that suggested complete understanding, and said, "Indeed it does."

The tension was thick. It was clear that the elderly man had resigned himself to his fate the very moment he refused to obey the king's laws. That is not to say, however, resigning one's self to a certain fate is the same thing as being comfortable with it. He did not want to die. He still had many years in front of him. He was very diligent, and incredibly wise. Indeed, his keen understanding of the world was the very thing contributing to his early departure from it. Because of his understanding of life, its purpose, and its meaning, he was now staring down the mouths of four very hungry lions—all with their own understanding of life's purpose.

As he sat in the small corner of the den, waiting for the feasting to begin, he found himself closing his eyes, thinking about an earlier, less complicated time. Though he had spent much of his life as an outcast, a foreigner in a strange land, he took pleasure in the memory of a life with his family that he left long ago. He could barely remember them, yet he had hoped to one day be able to return to what, if anything, was left of his home. He set aside those hopes when he refused to obey the king, and now his—

"Time's up!" shouted the little cub. "Seriously, that was at least five minutes plus forever and some more."

"'Forever and some more' little Leo?" smiled his mother.

"I'm not 'little Leo' anymore! I'm like four and a half months old now. Sheesh. So, are we going to eat him or what? Mom? Dad? I'm kind of hungry over here."

The leader of the pride glanced at the old man, and then back to his son, who, like the rest of them, had not eaten in days. He sighed heavily, "It's your call Lucy. If you think we should—"

"Leave him be," said Lilly. "He's done nothing to harm us. He's different than the rest of his kind. I can't quite put my claw on it, but he is just, I don't know, somehow different. Come on, we can live another day without eating, and, if we don't . . . well, so be it. Some things are worth dying for, huh?"

Without waiting for a response, Lilly walked back to the other side of the dark and musky den. She nestled down in a little groove on the floor and waited for the others to follow, which, after a moment or two, they did. A few hours went by and upon finding him completely unharmed, the delighted king freed his old friend from the den.

The next day the lions ate well.

4
The Honeymooners

"Sweeeeeeet," said Desmond with an extended satisfied tone befitting a creature with such a long tongue and neck.

"Why thank you, my dear," countered his oh-so-lovely wife Molly.

"Not you, honey." Desmond quickly recovered from his momentary lapse of reason: "I mean, of course you my sweet, spotted one," for Giraffe's really are of the kind sort, "but also this, check it out."

As Molly came closer, four of their best friends, Zooey and Pearl (two class-act zebras), as well as Grant and Alison (two class-act antelopes), also came in for a peek. You see, zebras and antelopes love giraffes. Now, there are many "official" and "documented" reasons that attempt to explain why zebras and antelopes love giraffes. Some suggest that it is due to the giraffe's ability to help pick the choicest fruits from the trees for their friends. Others suggest it is the giraffe's ability to see danger coming from a long ways a way.

I think, and this is just me, it has to do with the fact that a giraffe has a heart that is more than 2 feet long and over 20 pounds in weight! That's a big heart. Everyone knows that creatures with big hearts are easy to love. But, again, that's just my opinion.

"What's it say, Desmond?" asked Grant. "Tell us. What's it say?"

"Give him a chance," said Alison. "He's waiting for Zooey and Pearl to get closer, too." Alison loved Grant, but sometimes Grant was a bit impatient. Grant loved Alison because she was so patient, and for other reasons too.

"Okay, okay," said Grant. After about two seconds he asked, "How about now, Desmond?"

"Sure Grant. This is what it says: 'Come one, come all.'"

"That's it?" asked Zooey.

"Yep, 'fraid so. No, wait a second, someone marked out the one . . . it says 'Come two, come all.'"

In a somewhat sarcastic, but, only in a just-kidding kind of way, Zooey said, "Oh, that's much better." Despite his kidding around with Desmond, or perhaps because of it, Pearl gave Zooey a swift kick to the backside. Don't worry, it was a playful kick—all Pearl kicks are playful kicks. As a matter of fact, can you guess what zebras call playful kicks?

Pearl kicks.

"Sorry, Desmond, just giving you a hard time, buddy. But, why does that have you so excited?"

"Because," responded Desmond, "when was the last time just the six of us were able to 'come two, come all?'"

"That's a fine point you make," said a very serious Grant. "I can't seem to remember a time since, well, since the last time we went to a 'come two, come all' event. When was that again Alison?"

"It was last time."

"Oh yeah. Remember Desmond? It was last time."

"That's what I'm saying," said Desmond, even though he was no longer sure what anyone was saying. "That was the last time, which was a long time ago."

"So long ago," commented Grant, "that I can't even re-member going."

Everyone stood in a circle for a short while trying to re-member the last time they attended a "come two, come all" shindig.

Apparently, it was a long time ago, but none of them could quite put their hooves on exactly when. Fortunately, Molly interrupted the silence with a very important question: "So where is it that we are supposed to 'come two, come all'?"

"Yeah, Desmond, do you know?" asked Pearl. "Since you are the tallest one here perhaps you could tell us."

Pearl loved that Desmond was the tallest of their group, especially since she was the shortest. She was even shorter than Grant and Alison. You see, Pearl's mother was a Cape Mountain Zebra and her father was a Zony. So, that made here a Cape Mountain Zony. She thought this was pretty amazing because you just don't see those every day. For this group, that was always a major cause for celebration.

Animals love diversity.

I think that is another reason antelopes, zebras and giraffes get along so well—no two are alike. If you look closely at the stripes and spots on zebras and giraffes, each one of them is different; unique in their own special way. For some creatures, this might be a reason for silliness, but not for this bunch. For them, being different means (to quote a quartet of their favorite insects, the beetles)

"love, love, love."

Now, where were we?

Oh yes, the beauty of being short.

Not only was Pearl crazily unique because of her parents own diverseness, but she was very short. This brought her much happiness since she enjoyed catching rides with larger creatures. Her size gave her close friends Alfred and Ellen, who just so happen to be elephants, an opportunity to provide her with rides across the deeper parts of the river. Alfred and Ellen enjoy doing it so much that they have to take turns. You may not know this, but elephants have hearts that can weigh up to 60 pounds and, well, I don't have to tell you what that means.

Getting back to Pearl's question, "Do you know where this event is taking place?"

"To be honest," answered Desmond, "I'm not 100 percent sure."

"How much percent sure are you?" asked Grant.

"Oh, I would say about 12. Yeah, about 12 percent sure."

"Good enough for me," said the ever impatient Grant.

"Well, let's wait a minute here," said Alison. "Desmond, perhaps you could scan the horizon for us. Tell us what you see."

"Yeah," added Zooey. "Maybe you could run up to the top of the hill and look around. Perhaps that would increase your percentage of sureness."

"Perhaps," thought Desmond to himself. Except he more than thought it to himself since he said it out loud. "I don't like being 88 percent not sure."

"None of us do," reasoned Grant.

"Grant you just said . . . aw forget it," sighed Zooey.

As Desmond walked up the hill everyone enjoyed watching him sway onward as only a giraffe can sway. Desmond and Molly have a sort of swagger in their gait. Giraffes are very unusual in the manner in which they walk—yet another cause for celebration.

As Desmond approached the top of the hill, the excitement was about to overcome him. What would he see when he reached the top of the hill? Since he couldn't remember their last "come two, come all", he had no idea what to expect. Nevertheless, he was convinced it would be nothing but great. There would be food, friends, surprises and good times to go around for all. Of that, he was sure.

Alas, as he had reached the top of the hill and his excellent peripheral vision kicked in, he almost couldn't believe his eyes. "Why, it appears to be a parade!" Desmond shouted to himself.

Desmond loves parades. But, then again, who doesn't?

"Oh, Molly will be so pleased to know that there is a parade in town. And, why look, there are Alfred and Ellen! Wait just a second, who is that sitting on their trunks? Ah, it's Mango and Duncan! Look at those crazy lovebirds. Those two are always together, and I suppose they always will be.

"Oh, hey, there are Chocolate and Jiminy. Wow, it's been an eternity since I last saw those two. Who said a Welsh pony and a quarter horse couldn't make it work? Wait, is that . . .? No, it can't be. But it is, it really is! It's Kramer and Ginger! I thought those two had moved, but there they are, walking oh-so-happily together. I bet they're sharing millet seeds and yogurt drops. I know that sounds weird," said Desmond to himself, for he was a bit funny that way, "but that's because you don't know Kramer and Ginger. Oh, I can't wait to tell Molly. She has so missed them."

Without another thought, Desmond swaggered back down

the hill as fast as he could. When the others saw him galloping towards them, excitement consumed their imaginations. Especially Grant. He was tired of not being excited, so he was the first to get excited.

"What did you see?" screamed Grant.

"A parade unlike any other is what I saw!"

"A parade?" asked Pearl.

"Oh yes, a fine one, indeed. Perhaps maybe even the finest of parades, for guess who was there Molly! Just guess!"

Molly loved seeing Desmond so animated. "I don't know Desmond, who?"

"I saw . . . hold on . . . you know what? I bet they were going to the 'come two, come all' as well. It only makes sense. They love 'come two, come all' events. That's it! I know where it is. Let's go!"

On that note, everyone ran as fast as they could in the direction of the parade. As they drew closer they noticed hundreds and hundreds of pairs of all their friends. This had to be the legendary "come two, come all" affair because all were there and they were all there in twos.

As they approached the path of the parade they saw one of their oldest friends, Misty. Misty was a female whiptail lizard. Female whiptail lizards are so awesome.

"Hey Misty," said Molly, "are you heading to the parade?"

"Yes I am," exclaimed the eager lizard in her lizardish-type voice (which, by the way, sounds like a whisper combined with a loud shout). "Except, this is not just a parade we are joining, it's a honeymoon cruise!"

"Hooray!" shouted the gang. Honeymoons are great. Even though everyone had already been on their own honeymoons, they were informed that this was to be a special honeymoon cruise courtesy of some extraordinary guy named No Way.

"No Way?" asked Desmond.

"Yep," said Misty, "his name is No Way."

In a rather suspicious yet humorous tone Zooey confided his true thoughts on the subject, "no way."

"Way," responded Pearl.

"He even built the boat for us," added Misty.

Zooey noticed that Michael, Misty's best friend, was missing. "Where's my main man Mikey?"

"Oh, he and his brother are visiting their father and uncles. Guys night out you might say."

In an inquisitive tone, Grant asked Misty, "I thought this was a 'come two, come all' event, not a 'come one, come all'?"

"It is, but in this one instance No Way said it was okay."

"Well, I think that's great," smiled Molly.

Everyone agreed.

As the parade progressed, and more and more of the gang's friends showed up, everyone could barely contain their excitement. No one had ever taken a trip quite like this before. As soon as they discovered that the cruise was going to be for a whole month, maybe even longer, all the creatures became super-ridiculously happy. Just imagine, more than a month sailing with all of your best friends. It was hard to imagine, but everyone pulled it off.

"What a sweet thing to do for us," commented Molly.

"Yes it is," said Desmond. "I can't wait to meet and thank this Mr. No Way."

On this point everyone, yet again, agreed. They all concluded that in terms of having big hearts, this No Way guy must have the biggest heart of all.

5
Making History

"I am going to need a full statement from you."

That's Constantine. He's the resident stallion. He has the shiniest black coat I have ever seen, and he is also the only Friesian at Royal Stables. Rumor has it he was imported from some place called the Neverlands . . . or something like that. I don't know. To be honest, I don't really care where he came from, I just wish he would go back. Everyone at the barn, or, excuse me, the livery, as Julian the Dartmoor Pony calls it, agrees. Well, not everyone, maybe not even most everyone; but at least a few of us do. He just thinks so highly of himself. It's bad enough that some of our caretakers act this way, but now the horses are imitating them. Where does it end?

"But I already gave my statement, like seven other times."

That's George. George has it kind of rough around here. He's kind of short, gray, and his ears are big. I mean, really big. All donkeys have big ears, but his, well, they're really big. Put that together with his short body, and let's just say he doesn't get much respect around here. Now, in my mind, I think donkeys are pretty great. They have such a long history filled with interesting stories. Unfortunately, I may be the only one, besides Sabina, who thinks so. Sabina is an Arabian. I think she is the loveliest thing ever.

"I guess that means you are going to have to give it eight times, huh? If I want to hear it again, then I am going to hear it again. Because, you know what George, something is just not adding up with your story. I have to admit, it has me a bit confused. So, I think I'm going to need to hear it again."

At this point, it's pretty clear that Constantine is not going to let up. I mean, the whole place is watching. There's no way Constantine is going to let George off the hook.

"Yeah, donkey, tell us what happened or you're going to get it."

Great. Now Diocletian is getting in on the act.

"I said, tell us, you . . . you . . . fonkey donkey! Ha-ha-ha-ha-ha-ha! Fonkey donkey. That's hilarious. I said 'fonkey.'"

"That's not even a word, Diocletian."

"Sure it is George. Everybody knows it's a word. Isn't that right, guys?"

I look around. There's Trajan, Titus, Max, and Philip. Trajan and Titus are like Diocletian in that they are draft horses—shires to be exact. That means they're some of the biggest horses you'll ever see. Max is a Tennessee Walker (don't even ask how he ended up here), and Philip is like Sabina in that he, too, is an Arabian. That's pretty much the only quality those two share.

"I said, 'Isn't that right, guys?'"

The herd all agree with Diocletian. It's official. "Fonkey" is now a word. When you're one of the draft horses, your word is pretty much law.

"I said you better tell us or—"

"Diocletian," interrupted Constantine, "I can handle this.

Is that okay with you?"

Despite the fact that Diocletian is a Shire, he's not about to mess with Constantine. Constantine is not only strong, but he's fast. He also has something that Diocletian lacks: barn smarts.

"Sure, sure, yeah, absolutely. I just thought that I would, you know, I just thought that uh—"

"Therein lies the problem Diocletian, you were attempting to think. Now, if you please," continued Constantine, "I would have you to back up. I am quite sure I can handle this situation."

The big Shire dropped his head and moved back a few steps. He's embarrassed, but he figures it's better than Constantine rearing and striking him a good one. I don't think anyone around here would argue with that.

"Now, as I was saying, I need to hear, again, exactly what happened," repeated Contantine. "There is no point in being stubborn about it. Though, I am well aware that stubbornness runs in your bloodline, so I understand that you can't really help it."

"Stubbornness does run in my bloodline," said George. "My great grandmother, Jenny, they told her she wouldn't be able to have foals, but she proved them all wrong. Apparently, she got her stubbornness from her great grandfather. His name was—"

"No one cares about your grandmother's grandfather George."

"Actually, it was my great grandmother's great grandfather. You see, once he had to—"

"George, the only words I want to hear coming out of your mouth are words of explanation. So, begin," demanded Constantine.

"Well, I was just minding my own business when suddenly everyone started throwing their coats on me."

"Back up a second, what were you doing there in the first place? You know the big city is off limits to you."

"I wasn't in the big city Constantine, at least not at first. I was just hanging out in the little village waiting for—"

"Which village?" asked Constantine.

"The one with all the olives. I was just out there waiting for my master to load me up and ship me out. Because, you know, that's what I do. I carry things. Important things."

George tries so hard to earn everyone's respect, but it's no use. They'll never accept him. It's pretty obvious in Constantine's sarcasm: "Sure George. You are such an indispensable asset to the team. We just couldn't make it around here without you."

"Hey, there's no reason to get smart with him," interrupted Sabina. "Why don't you just leave him alone?"

"Actually, Sabina, I cannot help but get smart with him, because I am smart," responded Constantine. "Now, why don't you just mind your own business?"

"Yeah, Sabina, why don't ya just mind your own business, huh?" added Max. "Just mind it, why don't ya? Or else I'll have to teach ya a listen. Unless you're to yeller to—"

"Stuff it Max," said Sabina. "You wouldn't be quite so tough without your mob. A bunch of glorified oxen is all you guys are, just doing what you're told."

I really do love Sabina. She is the only one with the guts to tell things like they are which, unfortunately, keeps her on the outs most the time. It's a strange thing, really. I mean, why does one always get in so much trouble when they tell the truth to important folks? I guess that's why it's so hard to do.

"Sabina, I think it would be wise for you to stay out of this," said Trajan.

"Trajan, you don't know the first thing about wisdom," Sabina said, defending herself once again. "If it wasn't for your keepers you wouldn't even know when to eat."

I don't think Trajan is really that bad of a gelding. He's just like so many of us, caught in the middle. I think he would like for things to be different, but it's too easy to just go with the flow. Everyone is too scared to buck the system.

"Seriously, could you guys stop kissing up to Constantine for five minutes?" asked Sabina. "It's pathetic. And if it's all the same to you, *Mister* Constantine, I think I'll stay right here. Despite the company, I like it here in the barn."

"Livery!"

"Whatever, Julian," muttered Sabina.

We do live in the finest of stables. When you belong to royalty, you don't suffer much. Granted, they keep you busy, and you are fairly expendable, but, in that regard, so are most other horses and donkeys in our position. At least we have nice large paddocks to graze in the mornings and afternoons, and cozy stalls to sleep in at night. Julian likes them so much, in fact, he stays in his stall all day. Despite the fact that he could leave, he just hides in there and occasionally pops his head out to remind us he does exist. I think he is worried that the herd will put him in the same category as George, so he just keeps a low profile.

"I think I will allow it Sabina," Constantine said. "After all, you might learn something."

Constantine's chorus starts neighing in agreement. This goes on for a few moments until he says, "Enough."

On cue, they go silent.

"Let's cut to the chase, George. You have a very simple job here. It's not complicated, it's very straightforward: you carry things from one village to the next. That's all you have to do. You don't have to think, you don't have to make decisions, you don't even have to know where you are going. All you have to do is walk where they lead you. Yet, last week it appears that you tried to rise above your station in life."

"I'm telling you guys the truth. I was just minding my own business when all of a sudden these guys, I don't know who they were, I never saw them before in my life, but they—"

"What did they look like George?" interrupted Constantine.

"Well, they were kind of dirty, a little bit smelly, and they kind of reminded me of camels."

"Camels?"

"Yeah, I mean, in the sense of how camels are kind of nomadic. Always on the go. That sort of thing," George explained.

"So, they were drifters?" Constantine asked.

"Maybe. I mean, I haven't seen any of them since then. To be honest, they looked like they may have even been homeless. Just really scruffy and worn-down."

"Like you, huh George?" laughed Philip.

"Yeah, sure," George said. "Whatever you guys say."

Constantine continued his interrogation: "Then what happened?"

"Well, they led me over to him and then, well, I gave him a ride."

"Why would you do that, George? No one has ever sat on your back before, with good reason, I might add," said Constantine. "Where would you even get the idea that you should give this guy a ride?"

"He looked like he needed it," George offered innocently.

"Oh, but it was really the grandest sight—when we walked into town everyone started throwing their coats on the ground for me to walk on. I have never seen that before. And then, people were waving branches around, and then there was singing and dancing, and, well, the rest is history, I guess."

Despite everyone coming down so hard on him, George gets really excited and doesn't think how his retelling would cause jealousy among the horses . . . until it's too late. Constantine's ears perk and he moves in closer to George's stall. I'm grateful that Constantine can't get to him.

"It is only history in the sense that it's in the past, George. You see, your *kind* does not get to make history. History is made by the strong, the powerful—those in charge. It is made by kings, Caesars, warriors, government officials, nobility, and stallions. It is not made by the weak, the lowly, those filled with resentment for their small and insignificant place in life. It is not made by creatures like you or the one you gave a ride into the city."

George dropped his head ever so slightly at Constantine's explanation of history. Unfortunately, his posture of humility did not slow Constantine's tirade.

"You do know what they did to him, don't you?" asked Constantine. "He died like the common criminal he was, and his death was ordered by my master. *My master!* And you, you betrayed your own stable by being seen in public with him. That is why they locked you up. You are an embarrassment to the Royal Stable. You made a mockery of everything we stand for, all because you thought you would give him a ride. Well, I guess it makes sense—a donkey cavorting with a peasant. He was nothing more than a manual laborer gone rogue, a mere commoner with grand delusions about himself. You see how pathetic all this is, do you not? For as much as your kind hate those in power, underneath it all, you really want to be just like us."

"I . . . I don't hate you Constantine," George said. "I don't hate anyone. And I'm not jealous of any—"

"Stop lying to yourself. You are a donkey who tried to move beyond your lot in life. Yet, you could not do any better than a treasonous criminal from Nazareth, could you? Honestly, what good has ever come from that city? Well, if your time in your stall doesn't teach you any better, then maybe what happened to him will be lesson enough."

I don't think any of us had ever seen Constantine so angry. For some reason, George's actions really got to him. We don't know why, but it did. Constantine continued staring at him for another moment or so, and then he turned and walked out. The herd didn't dare make a noise. They waited a few moments and then followed him out of the stable. Trajan briefly looked back. There was this strange look in his eye that suggested he wanted to stay, but he just couldn't. The rest of us just watched as Constantine trotted into his own private paddock while the herd made their way into their shared paddocks.

We sat there in silence. Sabina wanted to speak, but she didn't. What could she possibly say? Julian was still hiding somewhere in his own stall, finishing off whatever bits of grain he could find in his trough. It's unlikely that he even heard much of the conversation. As long as it doesn't involve him, he doesn't care.

And here I am: Augustus the Great. Now known as Augustus the Replaced. I prefer to think of it more as retirement, though I'm not really that old; just old enough to not be of much use to anyone. That's life I guess. Thing is, I was once like Constantine: strong, quick, and very arrogant. I was the stallion of Royal Stables. I, too, had a master much like Constantine's. Though their names were different, their strategies were the same: rule by force, intimidation, and show.

Then there came a different one, and let it be said that it was right here, out of my very own barn, or livery, that one of our own gave him a ride. Yes, they killed him, but what would you expect? When someone envisions a new order based on the opposite of which all things are built, you have to kill them. It's too bad, really. Can you just imagine the possibilities?

Ah, retirement must be making me a bit sentimental. I'm now relegated to writing down these words in hopes that maybe, just maybe, somebody will one day find them and understand that the way things are is the way things have always been, and always will be, unless we start behaving a little less like stallions and a little more like donkeys. Until then, I guess nothing will ever change.

6
An Upset Stomach

I've heard it said that if you find
yourself in a really bad place,
you should start a journal. It's
the idea that writing down your
feelings is therapeutic. You
know, that it would be good for
you? Well, I can't seem to locate a
pen or a piece of paper in this place, but, then again, what did you
expect? I just never thought this is what it would be like. I mean, I
didn't exactly have high expectations as to where I would end up,
given my running away like that, but I just didn't think this place
would be so, oh, I don't know . . . stinky. Sure, I assumed it would
be rather shadowy, unpleasant, and altogether quite terrifying, but
I didn't realize I would be spending eternity surrounded by such a
foul odor. Seriously, it smells like dead fish in here.

Since I can't write this down and it doesn't seem like I'll be
going anywhere anytime soon, perhaps I'll feel a little better if I just
record my thoughts in my head. That's sort of a redundant idea,
huh? My thoughts are already in my head. Where else would they
be?

Let's try feelings. I'll go over my feelings in my head,
because feelings don't live in your head. Except for when you hit
it really hard then suddenly your head doesn't feel so good, but I
think that's different. Okay, enough stalling, here it goes: My first
thoughts were, "This cannot be good." Yep, that was it. Pretty heavy
stuff, huh? Hey, I never claimed to be a poet, all right? What did

you expect? Shakespeare? Dickinson? Cough-ka . . . wait, that's not right, maybe it's Koff, no, Kaf, oh who cares? It's not like I have to spell it or anything.

By the way, am I crazy if I talk to myself? Am I crazy for asking myself if I'm crazy for talking to myself? Or, am I crazy for asking myself if I'm crazy for asking myself if I'm crazy for . . . you know what? It's official—I'm crazy.

Let see, oh yes, back to my first thoughts. I already covered those. My first thoughts *after* my very first thoughts, when I noticed the water racing toward me, were, "Here it comes. The big kabloowey; daisies and buckets and all that. Jay, my friend, this is the end. You've lived a good life, sort of, but now it's over. So long cruel world! I'll miss you. Goodbye. Ah, reeve ah . . . ah . . . dirt-cheese."

So, here I am, spending eternity all alone in this stinky shadowy place thinking about how it's all over, except, well, it doesn't seem to be all over. You know, like, actually over? But here I am thinking about how it's over, but apparently it's not *really* over; otherwise, I wouldn't be able to think about how it's not really over.

Maybe this is not the end. I mean, I don't feel ended. I feel the opposite of ended. But that just doesn't make any sense. Maybe I'm dreaming. "I was dreaming when I wrote this, forgive me if it goes astray." Sorry, prone to lyrical tangents. But yeah, maybe this is all a really bad dream! Although I have to admit, I have never had a dream this smelly before. I mean, this is bad. Maybe this is some kind of joke. Sort of like, "No Jay, you are not going anywhere, not even to your death until I am through with you." Very funny. Just when I thought I was done, somebody decided to pull a fast one. Yep, real funny joke.

I guess I deserve it, though. Really, what was I thinking?

As if, even if I did make it to that town, I would somehow escape. Is there any place on, under, or even in this world in which you could get away? Of course not.

Wait a second, if there is no place on, under, or even *in* this world that you could escape to, that means, aw man . . . that means I can even be found here! Be found? He already knows I'm here! What was I thinking?

I don't know, what were you thinking?

Who said that? Was that me, or was that you?

Who are you?

Must be me.

I'm seriously going crazy in here.

There's still hope. I just need to let it all out. I just need to say it like it is and hope for the best. Fingers crossed and all that. All right, here it goes:

I'm not asking for any help here. That doesn't seem right given that it seems you have already provided help. Granted, kind of smelly help, but I'm not complaining or anything. I just wanted to say that you were right, as always, and I was crazy (which we have already established) for thinking I could escape who I am, and who I am supposed to be, which is only possible because of who you are.

Hmm, that sounded pretty good, maybe I could be a poet?

Nope, nope, you're right, I'm not a poet, but what I am is what I will be if given another chance to be who you called me to be. (Now that was poetic!)

Well? Anything? Anything at all?

Nothing. Absolutely nothing. It figures. That's what happens when you try to strike a bargain.

I didn't want to do it anyways. So there. Guess that means I win, huh?

Whoa, what's happening? Aw, here we go again! Another earthquake! This place has them like every three hours or so. I just need to hang on, which is more difficult than that sounds because everything is so slippery and mushy in here.

Mushy. I like that word. Mushy. Mushy, mushy, mushy! Yep. It's a stellar word—whoa, this earthquake is a real doozie! Just hang on Jay, it will end soon. I'm sure it will go away.

I hope.

Just when I was turning this dump of a place into a home, an earthquake hits.

How does an earthquake happen here anyway?

But this doesn't feel like an earthquake. Of course, I have never been in an earthquake so I don't even know what they feel like, but . . . now that's strange, I feel like I'm being sucked far- ther down into this dark stinky, though a bit mushy I must say, abyss— no, no, wait, wait . . . now I'm going the other way! Now I'm being dragged to . . . to . . . hey, is that light I see? Is that a speck of light? It is! It's light! It's, it's actually daylight! Ah, it's the sun! "Here comes the sun, and I say, it's all—" . . . whoah . . . I'm, I'm . . . mov- ing really, really fast. That's weird. Actually, wait, it appears that I'm . . . flying? But I can't fly . . . can I?

Aaahhhhhhhhhhhhhhh!!!!

Thump.

Ouch. I think my backside just said "thump." That's kind of strange. Guess that happens when you crash land on a . . . a beach? Huh. I appear to be on a beach. I landed on a beach?

Excellent.

That's what I'm talking about. I landed on a beach! Yep, I must have done something right. I'm not really sure what happened back there, but, as always, I survived. "Oh, as long as I know how to love I know I—" Jay, stop it. Why does that song keep popping in my head? Who cares? The only thing that matters is that just when I thought things were at their worse good old me pulled myself through it again. Way to hang in there Jay! You're the best.

What is that over in the distance? Well, what do you know? It appears to be a quaint little town. Maybe they will help me out and hook me up with some food. I was getting a bit sick of those slimy weeds. I wonder if they have steak? Wow, actually it appears that they do have, wait a second . . . wait a second! You have got to be kidding me. I mean, seriously, come on, is that really Nin—

"So, hold on a minute," interrupted Gracie. "Go back a second. You mean to tell me you put up with that incessant rambling, not to mention poor vocal performances, for 72 hours straight?"

"Something like that," responded George. "Worst case of indigestion ever! He just went on and on like that for days. I tried to spit him out at least a dozen times, but he would not leave. Even when I finally did get rid of him, I could still hear him going on and on about himself. I swam away as fast as I could. Let me tell you something Gracie, consider yourself fortunate if you never have to go through what I went through. It was awful. I truly hope that is the last time I ever swallow a human being."

7

The Examined Life
(with apologies to much of Western Philosophy)

Journal Entry 1.13,

As a zoologist, I am exposed to all sorts of animal behavior. Much of it defies what we wish to classify as normal. Yesterday's incident was surely a good example of abnormal animal behavior. A lion knocked a man off his donkey and, rather than attack the donkey, or make a meal out of either one of them, the lion just sat there staring at both the man and the donkey—as if lost in deep thought. Though it is the case that the lioness is the hunter and males fight for territory (or lionesses), I cannot imagine why the lion would go to the trouble of attacking only the man, and not the donkey he was riding. Did the lion imagine the man was encroaching on his territory? Did he view only the human as a threat, but not the donkey? That would be my best guess. If that is the case, then we have much to learn from the path that the donkey treads.

It is both the lion's and the donkey's behavior after the attack, however, that has me most puzzled. They were both just sitting there staring at the person on the ground. Fearful for my life, but desperate to understand what was going on, I snuck in for a closer look. As I slowly drew closer, cautious for my life, I witnessed the most unusual thing: the lion and the donkey were talking. For posterity's sake, I have translated for future researchers, as best I know how, their conversation. It began with the lion:

"As I gaze upon my spoils and examine the havoc I have wrought, I am reminded of the great bard's, um, the great barred owl that is, famous inquiry: 'To hoot or not to hoot, that is the question.'"

"I don't know if that is *the* question," the donkey responded. "It certainly is a question. Actually, is it really a question? I mean, it sounds more like a statement. What makes it a question? Now that is a question. Maybe *that's* the question."

"Doubtful" responded the lion. "Actually it was someone very important, I don't know who, that claimed 'doubt' should be the foundation of one's life."

"Well, I doubt that," said the donkey.

"Perhaps you are right," conceded the lion. "Perhaps it is certainty which we seek. Ever since my daring escape from the oppressive chains of tyranny—"

"Nicely said."

"—I have discovered that my newfound freedom has come with a hefty price," continued the lion. "It was a French, um, a French poodle, I think, who once said, 'we are condemned to be free.'"

"So, is that why you escaped?"

"Oh, you simple donkey. No. I escaped so that I could know life to its fullest. But do we really ever know anything? What does it mean to know? Do I know that I do not know the things I need to know? How would I know? Do you know?"

"No," said the donkey.

"A philosopher who is not taking part in the discussion is like a boxer who . . . well, who never boxes—especially with its front paws."

"We donkeys sometimes box with our back hooves. I guess that's not really boxing . . . more like bucking. Bucking, boxing, same thing."

"Oh, but is it? Can any *thing* be the same *thing*? What is the same? What is difference? Sure, you're a donkey and I am a ferocious lion, but are we really all that different?"

The donkey quickly replied, "I'm going to go ahead and answer 'yes.'"

"No! If by difference you mean . . . dif-fur-ance.'"

"What's the difference?"

"Indeed. What is the difference?" the lion countered.

"No, between the two?" the donkey explained. "Other than you said the second one more slowly and with a French accent?"

"Did I really say it more slowly? Did I really say it with a French accent?" asked the lion. "Or, did you just hear it slower and with a French accent?"

"I could really use some carrots," said the donkey, who was growing weary of the lion's confusing questions.

"What do you mean by the word 'use'? What would you 'use' carrots for?"

"Probably to plug my ears," responded the donkey.

"Do you hear only what you wish to hear?" asked the lion.

"Only when I'm hungry."

"Is life not more than bread?" asked the lion.

"I wasn't talking about bread, I was talking about carrots. I really love carrots."

"Now that brings to mind a serious question. Perhaps the most serious question this ferocious king of the beasts can think of: What is love?"

"Baby don't hurt me. Don't hurt me. No more."

Oblivious to the donkey's stirring rendition, the lion continued: "Must love be mutual for love to exist? Can you really love that which is unlovable? Do you only love carrots because of how they make you feel? That would make your love a selfish love. Narcissistic even."

"Narc-a-sissy? Who you calling a sissy?" the donkey asked, feeling rather insulted.

"Or, is your love true love because the carrot cannot love you back?" the lion asked, ignoring the donkey's question. "This would make your love the apex of love for it cannot be returned. The carrot is not a genuine other—it is not a subject, only an object."

"I object to the way you are dealing with the subject," said the donkey.

"Your love is grounded in that which does not exist. Therefore, does your love even exist? Does anything exist? Do we exist?"

"Not for much longer if I don't get some carrots. But speaking of things that no longer exist," the donkey said, trying to get back to the original point, "why did you jump this guy?

"It is in my nature," admitted the lion.

"Always?"

"Most of the time."

"Hmm. Good to know. But, uh, you and I are friends, right?" the donkey cautiously asked.

"It was Aris the Turtle who claimed that 'friends are those who share common ideas as to what constitutes the good life.' Do you agree?"

"Do you?"

"Absolutely," said the lion.

"Me too," agreed the donkey. "But, why him?" looking to the man on the ground. "I still don't understand."

"To quote another wise creature, it was Blaze my pet owl who once told me that 'all human vices derive from a single cause: their inability to sit still.'"

"You notice," the donkey pointed out, "that I have been very still, right? I am the epitome of all things still. Look at me being still."

"Yes, stillness is a trait indicative of most donkeys," said the lion. "It has surely saved your life today. I wouldn't dream of harming you. As Albert the Camel once said, "An animal without ethics is a wild beast loosed upon this world."

"And a donkey without carrots is a hungry donkey."

The lion smiled, "Touché my good friend, touché."

End of transposition.

Concluding remarks:

After reading and re-reading, countless times, this copy of their conversation, I must agree with the great 20th century philosopher Wittgenstein who once said, "If a lion could talk, we could not understand him."

8
Imagine

"What's going on here?" asked the young boy. "I thought wolves and sheep were bitter enemies."

Without taking his eyes off the creatures before him, the stranger stoically responded, "Not so. Granted, for the longest time, wolves preyed upon sheep. Sheep were food for wolves. They were also food for lions, foxes, humans . . . a great number of creatures actually. But that's all changed now. Those days are no more."

"What's changed?"

Remaining distant from the boy, yet firmly drawn to the creatures, he said, "He came back."

"Who? Who came back?" asked the boy.

The stranger (a man who appeared to be in his thirties, or, maybe his eighties, it was very hard to tell), looked away from the wolf and the lamb, and, as he did, they disappeared. They were no more. It was as if he was playing a trick. This made the young boy very sad. Was it a figment of his imagination? Was it a dream? No, no, they were real, of that the he was sure. The strange man must have done something with them, he thought. But before he could protest, the stranger gently offered his hand and said, "Would you care to see more?"

Under no obligation, the boy took his hand and found himself climbing a mountain. He had no idea how any of this happened. The last thing he remembered was sitting in his bed reading stories about owls, rabbits and kangaroos, and the next thing he knew, he was looking out of his window at a wolf and a lamb talking about bread, politics, and something or another. And now, after

grabbing the man's hand, he finds himself climbing a large mountain. Though he was only wearing his pajamas, since he didn't have
time to change into more appropriate clothes, he was, nevertheless,
oddly comfortable. He wasn't able to put on any slippers, yet his
bare feet felt nothing as they climbed higher and higher. It was as
if the   two of them were somehow scaling
                                    the mountain without touching it.
                                    "Where are we going?" asked the
                                boy.
                                    "Only to the end."
                                With a start, but not a word, the boy
                                    anxiously looked at
                                    the man. His re-
                                    sponse worried him.
                                    "Do not fear," urged
                                    the stranger. "The end
is remarkably similar to the beginning, as it must be."
        The boy was not sure why, but this calmed him greatly.
Even so, he remained focused on this old but ageless man. He kept
watching his eyes. If you were to ask the boy what color they were,
he would not be able to tell you. He would, however, tell you that
they seemed, for lack of a better word, troubled. It was as if they
were full of both life and death, yet were capable of neither.
        Feeling uneasy staring into a pair of eyes that had not yet
looked into his own, the boy looked down, only to realize that the
mountain was no longer beneath them. This frightened him, but,
as he raised his head, he saw that the mountain was, once again,
at eye level. Out of curiosity, the boy looked up. There was nothing. Again, he looked straight ahead and there was the mountain.
It was neither below him nor above him, but it was always in front

of him. This is something the boy, as he grew older, would never forget.

As they continued to climb higher, or seemed to climb higher (the boy was no longer sure), scenes of utter beauty would appear only to dissipate moments later. Every second they continued to rise, he noticed more and more flowers, lush trees bursting out of the mountainside, large bodies of cool clear water, and dense

patches of green playing host to creatures never found in his world.

The boy's attention fell back on the stranger's eyes. He was not sure if those eyes were responsible for creating everything he was momentarily seeing, or if the stranger's eyes were merely remembering something that was, or could have been, long ago.

He could not tell for sure.

As he was about to inquire into all these things, he suddenly had a feeling of peace and warmth that made him forget his questions. He felt like he was in the middle of the sun, yet without the fear of catching fire. Yet, when he last looked at his clock, before their departure to this new world, it was close to 10p.m.—a full hour after his bedtime.

"How is it that the sun is out?"

Staring straight ahead, the stranger replied, "That's not the sun."

"But how—"

"We are all formed by the same material are we not? The earth and all the creatures that come from it, we are all but specks of accumulated stardust. We are, in some vague but no less real sense, stars. Some of us realize this, and that enables us to burn brighter than others. Yet, this also leads to our fall."

Though he sensed he should appreciate what the stranger was saying, he felt the need to ask for clarification. "Excuse me? I'm not sure I understand."

"All stars burn out eventually."

"Yes, I guess so," the boy said. "I have seen a falling star or two. I always thought it was the most beautiful sight."

"Not for the star," the stranger pointed out.

Their conversation was suddenly interrupted by a vision of a peculiar sort. Directly across from them, as they hovered in nothingness, were many groups of animals. At first, the boy seemed unfazed, until he realized that he was looking at all kinds of animals, different species from different regions on the world, living peacefully together. He immediately noticed: leopards, geckos, bison, tapirs, warblers, leatherback turtles, lions, bears, komodo dragons, great horned owls, pigs, gannets, sheep, Asian horned toads, midwife toads, oriental fire-bellied toads, all kinds of toads—and how did he know so much about toads, or, for that matter, any of these creatures? To be sure, there were thousands more, it was just too many to name.

What was distinctively strange about it all was that they were living peacefully with one another. They were sharing a mountain, and despite the large diversity of creatures, there were no battles for territory, food, or space. A leopard was darting around, playing happily with a young goat. A number of calves were sleeping next to some brown bears as the calves' mothers were bathing some of the bear's cubs. An ox was sharing its straw with a lion, as a lioness was playing tag with couple of porcupines. There were black-browed albatrosses resting on the snout of crocodiles, orangutans rolling on the ground with warthogs, a koala sharing a pound of leaves with a Tasmanian devil, a chinchilla napping on the back of a hippo, a slow loris catching a ride with a flying lemur, while capuchins, tamarins, galagos, indris, and red howler monkeys spent their time dancing in the surrounding warmth of it all. There was really just too much to absorb. The boy was on the brink of tears.

Feeling as if he were about to burst, he looked at his guide as he too gazed upon the scene. Through the course of their brief time together, the boy's host had, for the most part, appeared to be without emotion. Even now, he merely stared mechanically, perhaps lost in the moment. He showed no visible expression. Unlike the boy, there were no tears of happiness about to flood his face; there was only a look of emptiness.

"Why are you so sad?" asked the boy. "Does this not make you just the happiest person in the world?"

The mysterious stranger continued looking at the mountain that was so full of life. For the briefest of moments, he almost seemed to smile when a Bolivian squirrel monkey offered some fruit to a pearl-spotted owlet. He must have felt the boy notice his momentary lapse of vulnerability as he softly muttered, perhaps to himself, "Sometimes it is the sweeter things in life that break you."

As the boy started to ask what he meant by that, the man said, "Look over there."

The boy's eyes quickly looked in the direction suggested by his guide. He saw another young boy, only months, maybe weeks, younger than himself, sitting in the shade of an old baobab tree petting a snake (how he knew it was a baobab tree, he did not know). The snake was wrapping itself around his arms, not in a constricting manner, but with kindness and affection. The snake was hugging the child in the only way it could. The child was smiling and talking to the snake, though the boy could not hear his words.

"What are they talking about?"

"Something only they can hear."

As an act of kindness, the stranger added, "If I were to guess, something to do with the past, the present, and the future; something to do with this moment, their moment, not ours. You must understand, I cannot hear it either. As far as we are concerned, they might as well be silent."

The boy started to say something, something to suggest a lack of understanding, but decided against it.

Without taking his eyes off the child and the snake, the boy's guide said, "Silence is not always the best response, but sometimes it is the only response. We can only hear that of which we can speak, and we can only speak of that which we can see. Now, go to them. Though they will not be going anywhere, they will not be here long. Listen to them. Tell me, if you can, what you hear, or better, what you see."

The boy looked at his guide for further advice, but immediately knew there was nothing left to say. As he started walking to the child, he heard the man say, "Be sure to keep moving forward, I'll be right here. Everything will be as it should be."

Though the child and the snake appeared to be nearby, the closer he seemed to get to them, the further he seemed to be away from them. He really did not mind this, as with each step he took, he grew enamored by the millions, if not billions, of kinds of insects enjoying their life amongst one another. The cicada and the grasshopper, the butterfly and the fire ant, the praying mantis and the buthid, were all playing and sharing food with one another. There was absolutely no violence, tension, or struggle.

There was only peace.

Along the way, he desperately wanted to play and eat with the marsupials, rodents, insectivores, monotremes, and reptiles that occupied the passing mountainside, but he felt that it was imperative to ignore this desire. Oh, but what it would mean to lose one's self in this paradise. The idea of it was enough to send him running off the path in order to join the various species of primates in song and dance. Yet, he could still feel the stranger pushing him to continue forward.

After a few moments, or perhaps years (in this place it is very difficult to tell), he drew close to the child holding the snake. As he approached them, he noticed there were a wide variety of trees that surrounded them: oaks, pines, cedars, redwoods, spruces, sequoias, maples, weeping willows, firs, dogwoods, birches, magnolias, hickories, and so on. He had no idea that his knowledge of either the animal world or of trees was so thorough, but he was learning that there were lots of things that he knew, and even more that he didn't know. Sometimes it requires a lot of knowledge to know all that you do not know.

As he drew near, into the dense forest on the endless mountain, the boy felt as if he knew this child. He looked so familiar, yet at the same time like someone he was destined to forget. As he approached them, the snake started clinging tightly to the child. He was not trying to hurt the little child, rather, he was holding on for life. The snake seemed genuinely terrified by the intrusion of the two visitors.

"I mean you no harm," said the boy (who realized that his voice was suddenly deeper than only moments before).

"You never do," hissed the snake.

The child continued caressing the snake as if he were trying to calm it down. For the first time since this . . . this vision, or dream, or whatever this may be, the boy felt as if something was not quite right. He was sensing a tear in the seams of this perfect world, and he could not shake the feeling that it had something to

do with him. He also felt . . . older. Much older. Had he been here longer than he thought? He simply had no conception of time. It almost seemed like time did not exist, yet it was obvious that some creatures were older than other creatures. Had he aged since his arrival?

The boy who was becoming a man asked his guide, "What

is going on here? Why does the snake not trust me?"

"Because you are to lead them."

The young man who was growing even older looked at the stranger, who may be eighty, or thirty, there was no way to tell, and said, "What do you mean? What do you mean I am to lead them?"

For the first time, the stranger let go of his detachment from the boy and looked into his eyes.

It was not a consoling look.

"They existed before you, and in such existence they lacked knowledge of themselves. Despite their ignorance, however, or perhaps because of it, they were at peace. They knew nothing else. Then you came along and named them—as was your task. Yet, you did not name them well. You restricted your understanding of them in light of how it served you. How banal. For you did not need to do this in order to prove some sense of superiority over other animals. Your superiority would have been obvious had you chose a different path. Instead, all that you now see is little more than a haunting memory."

The man paused, as if he were looking inside himself for something, and then continued, "At times, it even seems to me to be unreal. But unlike you, I am not afforded the luxury of denial." The stranger, who only moments earlier seemed quite controlled, appeared be engaging in an internal battle. There was rage within him. Deep-seated rage. It had been there a long time, speculated the boy, and he could sense that the man was incapable of coming to terms with it. The boy pitied him.

The stranger took his eyes off his young but aging companion, and as if to look everywhere and nowhere, ominously grinned and asked, "Do you see what has been lost?" Somehow knowing what the boy was thinking the stranger added, "Who is to blame? In asking this question, you only commit yourself to my path."

As the boy who was quickly becoming a man looked into the stranger's eyes he could see the mountain and all of its residents. The mountain no longer existed beyond the guide, but only through his eyes. He watched them gather around the child. Everything from the cape ground squirrel to the white rhinoceros to the African buffalo had gathered around the little boy.

As the man looked deeper into the eyes of the stranger, he saw his former self, the boy, looking back at him. He could see himself looking at the child with the snake. The snake crawled up the child's arm and around his back in order to peek his head over the shoulder of the child. The little boy showed no fear; the snake was not so sure. As the boy become man continued to age, he could not take his eyes off the stranger's eyes. It was, indeed, a hypnotic gaze. He could no longer see anything but himself. The bears, the cows, the monkeys, they were all gone. There was no wolf lying beside a lamb; there were no lions eating straw. There was no mountain. There was only a very old man looking into a mirror realizing that he had let them all go. He suddenly became aware that the stranger was never in front of him, but behind him, peering over his shoulder.

Index of Scripture

Below are listed the scripture references used for each story.

Chapter 1: The King's Spider

I Samuel 17:34-54; 22:1; Proverbs 30:28 (This story also draws inspiration from extra-biblical Jewish commentary.)

Chapter 2: Twenty-Two Hands

Numbers 22:22-33

Chapter 3: Hunger Strike

Daniel 6:1-28; Acts 5:29

Chapter 4: The Honeymooners

Genesis 6:11-22; Proverbs 12:10

Chapter 5: Making History

Mark 11:1-2, 7-8

Chapter 6: An Upset Stomach

Book of Jonah

Chapter 7: An Examined Life

(with apologies to much of Western Philosophy)
I Kings 13: 23-28

Chapter 8: Imagine

Genesis 3:14-15; Isaiah 11:6-9

Tripp York

teaches at Western Kentucky University in Bowling Green, Kentucky. His other books include *The Purple Crown: The Politics of Martyrdom* (Herald Press), *Living on Hope While Living in Babylon* (Wipf & Stock), and *Anesthesia* (Seaburn Press). He also acts professionally, designs lights for the stage, and spends much of his free time with his blind Siberian Husky, neurologically-challenged cat, and very temperamental horse.

Zak Upright

is an illustrator of sorts and all around nice fellow. Being creative is the essence of this guy, having been an artist most of his life.

His illustration background ranges from comic books to commercial art to graphic design.

He resides in Durham, North Carolina with his wife, son and cat.